Thoughts THAT COUNT

Copyright © 2014 Authored by Byron Wesley Lehman
All rights reserved.

ISBN: 1500501956
ISBN 13: 978-1500501952
Library of Congress Control Number: 2014912620
CreateSpace Independent Publishing Platform
North Charleston, South Carolina

Thoughts THAT COUNT

BYRON WESLEY LEHMAN

Dedicated to my wife, Sherry; my four children, Ashley, Laura, Wesley, and Marissa; my five grandsons, Alec, Ethan, Davis, Emory, and Henry; and to my only granddaughter, Olivia.

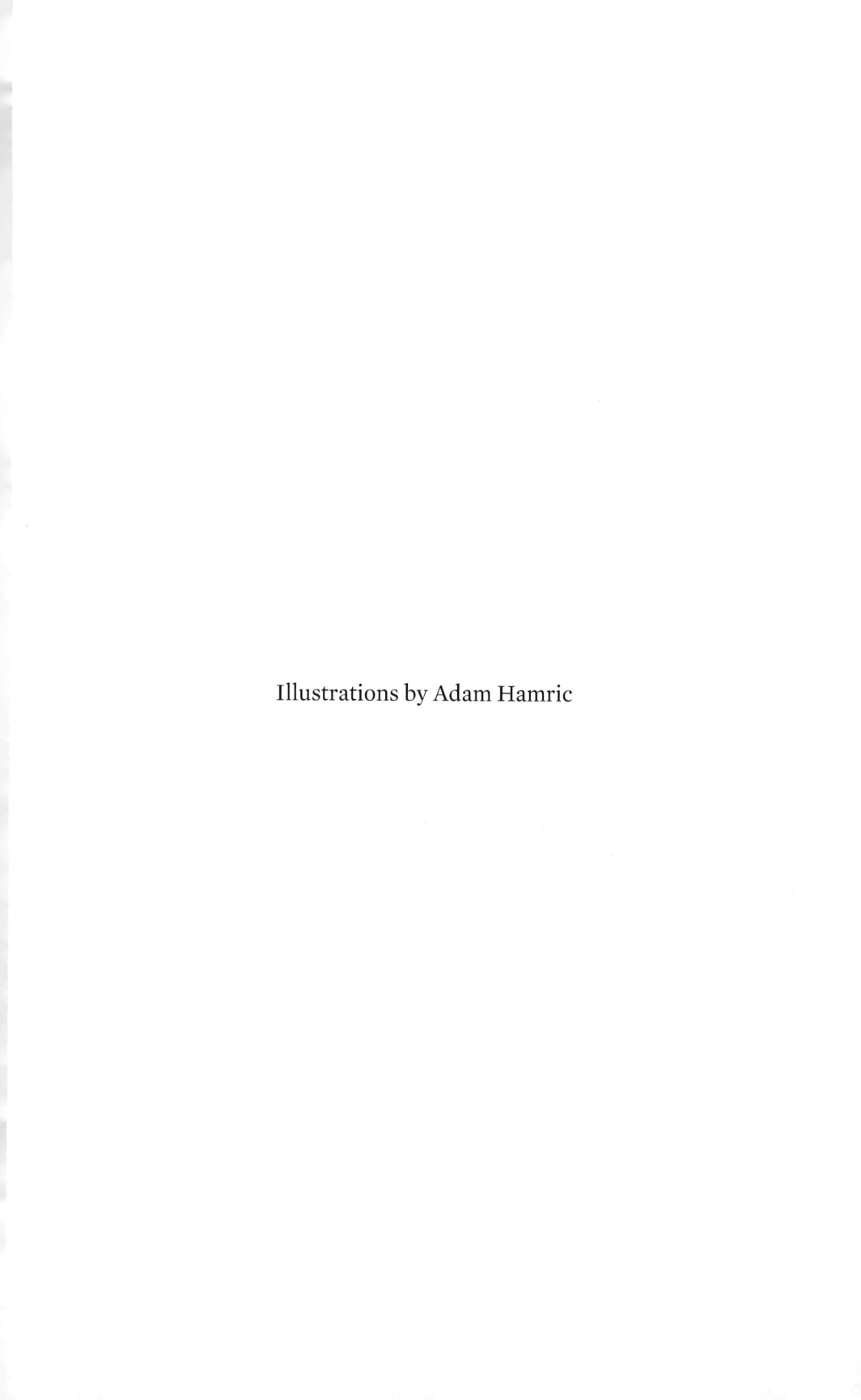

Illustrations by Adam Hamric

Foreword

Our approach to character development has been simple enough. We began by determining which principles of living we thought to be of greatest importance. For each principle selected, we then attempted to create the following:

1. A title and a one sentence statement of principle, either one of which, when shared between adult and child, could serve as a kind of shorthand to facilitate future discussion, allowing for the more effective use of what we often call "teachable moments"
2. A story or other explanatory text
3. An illustration which so clearly identifies the principle to be learned that it can stand alone as a tool for improving long-term retention

While experience may be the best teacher, we believe that prior exposure to effective living principles (a kind of preteaching) can do much to influence our children's interpretation of their life experiences. To use a simple analogy, a recording in Latin can be "experienced" (heard) by just about anyone. But unless that experience is preceded by the study of Latin, it is unlikely to produce understanding or new learning. Such an experience passes through our brain but finds nothing to stick to. In a similar manner, we believe that an early exposure to the principles of good character will affect young people's recognition of the events surrounding them and provide a sound basis upon which to evaluate relevant experience.

As you read the stories, refer back to the title or the statement of principle under the title. You can quickly remind yourself or your child of the important principle to be learned. For example, if your child leaves

Thoughts That Count

behind a mess in her room, you can remind her to check her "rearview mirror." Or when you are faced with one of life's many challenges, remind yourself that "hard-to-do things make you stronger."

Order of Presentation

1.	CHOICE	1
2.	CONSEQUENCES	3
3.	IN CONTROL	5
4.	LIFE ISN'T EASY	9
5.	LIFE ISN'T FAIR	11
6.	MORE	15
7.	THANKS GIVING	17
8.	W – O – R – K	19
9.	ONE NOW, OR TWO LATER?	21
10.	LITTLE RED WAGON	24
11.	THE COOKIE JAR	26
12.	ME-VILLE	29
13.	WHAT'S YOUR EXCUSE?	31
14.	TREASURE HUNT	34
15.	HARD-TO-DO THINGS	37
16.	SWING THE BAT	39
17.	GET BACK UP!	41
18.	DRAGONS	43
19.	THE TOOLBOX	47
20.	LIGHT ONE CANDLE	49
21.	SUPERHEROES	51
22.	BABY STEPS	54
23.	PROMISES	56
24.	SIZE OF THE DOG	58
25.	CHEERLEADER	60
26.	INVISIBLE	62
27.	THE REAL WORLD	65
28.	THE SAME BOAT	68

29.	UNDER CONSTRUCTION	70
30.	REARVIEW MIRROR	73

Choice

**You have the power to choose;
you control your own remote.**

How would you like to hold the remote controls to your own personal robot? Are you hungry? Send old Robo to the kitchen to fix you a snack, a full meal if you like. Does your room need to be cleaned? No one enjoys that; let Robo do it. Homework? Why give up your favorite television program to do what your favorite robot can do for you? Let's face it, the possibilities are endless. Robo does what he is told to do, and you control the remote!

Unfortunately, too many of us act as if we are the robot and our controls are in the hands of everyone we meet. We say things like, "He made me do it," or "She started it," to excuse our own bad behavior. When someone cuts in front of us in the cafeteria line, we become angry automatically, without thinking, as if the person cutting in line held our remote. Call us a name and our feelings are hurt. Having lost our temper, we explain, "He made me mad," as though we really had no choice. Why do we lose our temper? Because someone made us, as though we really have no choice. One person after another flips our remote this way and that, and we feel and act as if we have no choice, just like Robo. Sometimes, we are even controlled by events. A little bad weather, and we think our entire day is ruined, as though we are controlled by the weather. Fail even once, and we give up—automatically, without thinking.

But we are not robots. They have no choice; we do! They are controlled by others; we are not. No one else controls our remote; we do! In fact the freedom to choose how we feel and how we act is our most important freedom. When others cut in front of us, we *can* choose to be angry, but we can also choose to ignore them. We can laugh at the names we are

Thoughts That Count

called, if we choose. In fact, we can respond in many different ways, and the choice is ours to make. Bad weather doesn't have to ruin anyone's day, even if plans have to be changed. And almost no one ever becomes successful without first failing and choosing to try again.

Rather than accept responsibility for the choices we make and admitting our mistakes, we prefer to make excuses, to find someone else to blame. Someone else controls our remote. Every day we hear the excuses. If we listen carefully, we may even hear them from our own lips. Don't fall into their trap. Take responsibility for your own actions. Grab hold of your own controls. Though you can't always control what happens to you, you can almost always control (that is, choose) how you respond. Now, repeat after me: I am not a robot controlled by others, or by the things that happen to me. I control my own remote; I make my own choices.

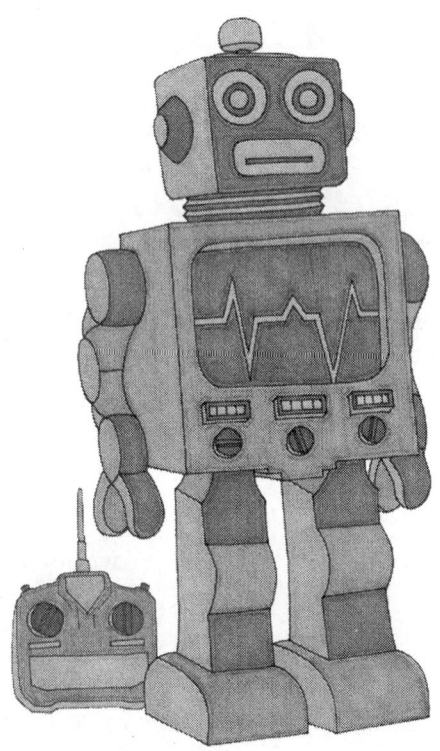

Consequences

Consider the consequences of the choices you make *before* you make them.

So, *you* have the power—the power to choose. No one else controls you; you control yourself. If you want to stick your tongue on a frozen flagpole, no one can stop you. If you want to eat all your Halloween candy at once, maybe you can. If you want to rub noses with a crocodile, well, you can try. No matter what happens around you, you are free to choose how you act or react. You can choose to tell the truth, or choose to lie. You can share with your friends, or keep it all for yourself. You can learn from your mistakes, or refuse to admit them. You can choose to finish your work, or choose to ignore it. The choice is yours to make. That's the good news.

But after the good news comes the bad: c - o - n - s - e - q - u - e - n - c - e - s. Every choice you make has consequences, and not all of them are good, like getting your tongue stuck to a frozen flagpole. Choose to tell the truth, and others will learn to trust you—a good consequence. But choose to lie, even sometimes, and their trust in you will die—not so good. Share with your friends, and they will share with you. But a selfish person will soon have no friends to share with. Learn from your mistakes, and you may never have to repeat them. But refuse to admit your mistakes, even to yourself, and you will make them again and again. Are the consequences better when you finish your work, or when you ignore it?

The problem is that we want to be able to make bad choices without suffering bad consequences. We want to eat our Halloween candy all at once, and not get sick. We want to be good at music or sports (or whatever), without having to practice. We want to stay up late, and not be sleepy at school the next morning. We want to believe that consequences don't exist, or that they exist only for others, not for us. We want to believe that we could play Frisbee all day in the middle of a busy street, and somehow never get hit by a car. We want our story to have a happy ending, no matter what choices we make.

The simple truth is, if you want good consequences, you have to make good choices. If you want others to trust you, you have to tell them the truth. If you want to keep your friends, you must learn to share with them. If you want to learn from your mistakes, you must first admit them. If you want credit for the work you have done, you must first do the work.

Like them or not, consequences do exist; you cannot escape them. Every choice you ever make will have them. So consider the consequences of the choices you make *before* you make them.

Oh, about that crocodile—find someone else to rub noses with.

In Control

If you want to control what happens around you, first control yourself.

Imagine sitting on your very own throne and commanding everyone around you. You make the rules and give the orders. Everyone else obeys. The kingdom is yours. You are the one in charge. You are the one in control. Never again will anyone tell you to eat your vegetables, do your homework, or be nice to your little sister or brother. You can go anywhere you want and do anything you like. Wow! How would you like to rule a kingdom like that?

Of course, in the real world, most of us will never find a throne to sit on or a kingdom to rule. But we do want to have *some* control over what goes on around us. Having no control would be like spending the rest of our lives watching someone else play a video game, when we all know it is more fun to have the controls in our own hands. So, if we can't be the boss of *everything, all of the time,* we would sure like to be the boss of *some things, some of the time.* We may want to convince a parent to buy something for us that we could not buy for ourselves, or persuade friends to go where *we* want to go and do what *we* want to do. We want to have our ideas listened to and respected. Someday, we might want to be the person in charge—someone like a schoolteacher or principal, the owner of a business, leader of a band, or manager of the New York Yankees. We might even have bigger dreams, like changing the world. Can anyone really change the world? Why not?

The problem is that we want to control other people without first learning to control ourselves—to be respected before becoming a person who deserves respect, to lead before becoming a person people want to follow, to have our ideas heard before listening to the ideas of others. But our ability to control what happens around us depends on our ability to control ourselves first.

What does it mean to control yourself? Do you ever get angry and do things you shouldn't do, or say things you shouldn't say? Most of us do, but we don't have to do it again—not if we learn to control ourselves. Do you watch what you eat? A lot of us don't. Can you control your thoughts and focus on the job before you? Can you make a promise and keep it? Can you work toward a goal until you achieve it? And what about your behavior? Has anyone ever told you you're out of control? What does that tell you? What habits do you have, both good and bad? Who controls them? You could, you know. And here's a good one: Do you control your fears, or do they control you? Fear can keep us from doing really dangerous, harmful things. But it can also keep us from doing just about *anything*, including a lot of things we could be doing if we had the courage to try.

How do you learn to control yourself? One answer is practice—the same way you learn to play a musical instrument, or learn to do just about anything else. Opportunities for practice are not hard to find. How long has it been since you were last tempted to lose control, to react with anger, to strike back, or act without thinking? Probably not long. Welcome each such opportunity, though it may seem unpleasant at the time. You can also learn to control yourself by changing your habits, one by one. Maybe you could start by getting enough sleep at night, being more responsible about what you eat, paying more attention to the words that come out of your mouth, or making only the promises you can keep.

So, if you want to rule a kingdom, begin with the Kingdom of You. If you want to be the boss of everybody, first be the boss of yourself. Set your own goals and stay with them. Set your own limits so no one else has to set them for you. Control your emotions. If you want to control what happens around you (to be the one in charge, to lead, to have influence, to make a difference), first learn to control yourself.

Byron Wesley Lehman

Thoughts That Count

Life Isn't Easy

Life isn't easy. It isn't supposed to be.

Do you like *difficult*? Not everything difficult is easy to like, but like it or not, life *is* difficult. As young children, most of us found our way into the saddle of a carousel horse or two. Up and down and around we go—a great ride, even if we didn't get to "go again," as we had hoped. But as we soon learn, life is no carousel ride. Life is more difficult, more like riding a bronco, with lots of bumps and plenty of falls along the way.

Being lonely is hard. Being sick is hard. Going hungry is hard. (Most of us have no idea just how hard that would be.) For some of us, taking a math test is hard. Sometimes telling the truth is hard. Being lied to isn't easy, either. Admitting our own mistakes is hard. Nobody likes to lose; nobody likes to be disappointed. Someday we may have to work hard day after day to support our family. That's hard, too.

Yes, life is difficult. If your ride isn't bumpy now, hold on tight; it will be soon enough. Our biggest problem, though, isn't the rough ride; the problem is that we *expect* a smooth one. So, when the bumps occur, two things happen. First, we feel sorry for ourselves, as though we are the only ones ever to experience difficulties. Then, soon after, we look for someone to blame—parents, friends, teachers, anyone will do.

The *good* news is this:

1. Life gets easier when we understand that the ride is bumpy for everyone, not just for us. Rich people are as likely as anyone else to have their feelings hurt, their hearts broken, their dreams shattered. Even doctors sometimes catch the flu. Are you the first person ever to cut your finger? Drop something on your foot? Work late, or get up early?

2. Life also gets easier when we learn to make good choices. After all, many of the difficulties we face, we create for ourselves. The ability to make good choices depends, in part, on how much we learn from the bad choices we have already made. Our mistakes teach us what doesn't work, and lead us to something that works better. So, learn the lesson each bumpy ride has to teach—the bumpier the ride, the greater the lesson to be learned.
3. Finally, life gets easier when we realize that we *need* to be challenged. We humans are made for the bumps. Imagine riding on a carousel for the rest of your life. Sure, you would have fun for a while. But you wouldn't get anywhere, and you would soon become bored with the ride. Once you have mastered a video game, do you really want to play it over and over again? Or wouldn't you rather move on to a new, more challenging game? Truth is, we humans are made to be challenged. We are made for the bronco, not the carousel.

When the ride gets really rough, you may want to ask, "Why did this or that have to happen to me?" You won't always understand why, but fortunately, you won't have to. When you begin to accept as normal the difficulties and challenges of life, you can focus on ways to make your life better, rather than feeling sorry for yourself or finding someone to blame.

Life can be wonderful, but it won't be easy. It isn't supposed to be. Maybe someday you too can say, "This is difficult, but I like difficult."

Life Isn't Fair

Life isn't fair. We aren't all given the same things, and we don't all have the same chances.

Have you ever heard a child say, "If you don't play fair, I'm not going to play anymore"? Have you ever heard someone complain about not having something someone else has? How could that be fair? At one time or another, we have probably all had the feeling that the "game" of life just isn't fair. Well, the truth is that life *isn't* always fair—not for you, not for anybody. Is it fair that some children are born into great wealth, while others don't have enough to eat? Is it fair that some of us are healthy, while others suffer from terrible diseases?

For every person like you, there is a Mary and a Sam, people who seem to have an unfair advantage. They may have nicer clothes, a bigger house, or more "toys." Perhaps they are smarter or more talented. They might have fewer obstacles to overcome, or a family that can do more to help them. You probably know someone like them, though their names probably aren't Mary or Sam. The simple truth is that we don't all start even in the game of life. Some of us have a better chance of succeeding than others. So what do you do if you do not have the advantages that others seem to have? Quit? If you do, you will have NO chance of succeeding. Do you refuse to play until the game is somehow made fair? If so, you may have a long, long wait.

Now for something you may never have considered before: for every person like you, there is also a Bill and a Sue. Though we are quick to feel sorry for ourselves and point to those who have more than we have, we seldom think about those who have less. If you are in good health, a citizen of the United States, sleeping with a full stomach and a roof over your head, you are far more fortunate than most. Now think about it.

Thoughts That Count

When was the last time you worried about fairness when you had more and someone else had less? When was the last time you thought, "This isn't fair; I have so much more than he has or she has?" If we are honest, nearly all of us would have to admit that the "unfair" world we live in doesn't always favor others; sometimes, it favors us.

Fortunately, life isn't just a game of chance. Our success doesn't depend on a lucky spin, but rather on doing the best we can with whatever chances we are given. Frederick Douglass was born a slave. Was that fair? Of course not. But after gaining his own freedom, Douglass, a true American hero, worked to rescue other slaves and bring about the end of slavery in America. Abraham Lincoln's mother died when he was only nine. How could that be fair? Franklin Roosevelt suffered from polio, a disease seldom seen today. Of course, both Lincoln and Roosevelt later became presidents of the United States. Poet John Milton wrote his most memorable poem after he had gone blind. Musical composer Ludwig van Beethoven wrote his greatest symphony after becoming deaf. All of these people faced hardships most of us will never face, but though all died long ago, their names and accomplishments are still honored today. Many, many others, some famous, some not, have similar stories to tell.

Fairness is a good thing. We should all try to treat others fairly and defend those who are treated unfairly. But don't let the lack of fairness become an excuse for not trying. Too many of us fail to achieve what we could, fail to reach our potential, because we refuse even to try until somehow, magically, everything is made fair. If you wait for fairness in the game of life, you will be waiting for the rest of your life, and wasting the opportunities you are given.

The absence of fairness can also become an all-purpose excuse for failure: "It wasn't my fault." "I didn't have a chance." When we focus on things beyond our control, including fairness, we often ignore what we *do* control, what we ourselves could be doing better. In other words, thinking about things we cannot change only keeps us from changing what we can.

Sometimes life really isn't fair. Play the game anyway. Someone may have something you don't have, but that doesn't mean you should have it, too. And not having something now doesn't mean you can't *earn* it later. Whether you are among the most fortunate or the least, your task is the same: not to compare yourself to others, but to make the best possible use of whatever blessings, talents, and opportunities you are given.

Thoughts That Count

More

**No matter how many "toys" you have,
they will not make you happy; you will always want more.**

Brandon and Brooke were twins who lived in a nice home with two parents who just couldn't say "no." When Brandon wanted a new baseball glove, he got a baseball glove. When Brooke wanted a stuffed giraffe, she got it. Eventually, their "toys" outgrew their toy box, so their Dad built a bigger box. About that time, Brandon saw a new train set at Jake's house that could do tricks his train couldn't. So, of course, he wanted one, too. Meanwhile, Brooke had seen a new board game advertised on television. She seldom played board games, but perhaps she would like this one better. Before long, even their new toy box was filled to overflowing. Were they happy now? Not yet. An even larger box would have to be built...

To make a long story shorter, walls were eventually torn down and ceilings removed to allow for a toy box big enough to hold all the toys that Brandon and Brooke thought they wanted. An elevator was built to take the twins to and from the top of the box, where a family of elves would provide them whatever toys they desired at the time. The elves, of course, were also responsible for picking up the toys and returning them to the box after Brandon and Brooke had finished playing. (Brandon and Brooke, it seems, weren't responsible for much of anything.)

Eventually, a giant screen was added to one side of the box, so the twins would have cartoons to watch while playing. Remote controlled this-and-thats were everywhere—from monster trucks to motorbikes, fiery dragons to fire trucks, robots to race cars. Since only space-age batteries were used, the twins knew that no battery would have to be replaced before the two of them turned sixty. Oh yes, their toy stove actually worked, making it possible for the elves to prepare burgers and

Thoughts That Count

fries anytime the twins were hungry. With so many toys to choose from, the twins rarely went outside to play with friends. And schoolwork? They had no time for that. Surely now the twins were happy, right? Not yet.

"Aren't the kids with the most toys supposed to win?" Brooke wondered. "We have the biggest toy box in the world. Why aren't we happy?" Brandon, of course, had no answer.

Everything Brooke and Brandon wanted, Brooke and Brandon got. They never had to work for what they wanted. They never had to wait, and never experienced the joy of getting something they had worked and waited for. Nor did they learn to be happy with what they already had, a lesson we all need to learn.

Life is not a giant toy box and the purpose of living isn't to fill our box with as many toys as possible. Clothes, houses, cars, jewelry, toys of whatever kind—these things aren't bad, but they won't make us happy. A new toy *does* bring a moment of pleasure, but a part of us will always want more—like a child on Christmas day after all the gifts have been opened. Brooke and Brandon did not understand that we humans are bigger than our toys, bigger than all the things money can buy. To be happy we need things money *can't* buy. We need to love and be loved. We need to be challenged, to have goals to work toward. We need to feel needed. We need to experience success, to solve problems, to believe that our lives have meaning and purpose. Without these, all the toys in the world won't make us happy. What better time to learn than now, for unlike the Brooke and Brandon of our story, you will *not* be getting everything you ever wanted. In the real world, no one ever does.

Thanks Giving

**Give thanks every day for what you have
and what others have done for you.**

No matter how much we already have, most of us could think of a lot more we wish we had—a bigger bedroom, a million dollars, a dog or a cat, new clothes. What is on your wish list? Does your list include a few things you already have, but wish you didn't, like a kid who makes fun of you at school, or chores at home? (Now there's a good one.) But be careful what you wish for. The story is told of a young boy who wished he didn't have such a funny-looking nose. He got his wish, all right. When he awoke the next morning, he had no nose at all.

    A wish list can be a good thing, especially if you are willing to work for the things you want. But hopefully, you have another list as well, at least in your mind—a list of things for which you are thankful. Chances are that list would be a long one, if you thought for just a while. Are you thankful for the gift of life, or do you take it for granted? How about good health? Are you thankful for your friends and family? For your favorite foods or your favorite songs? How about the freedoms you enjoy? Are they on your list, or have you even thought about what life would be like without them? For even the least fortunate among us, the list goes on and on. You might also be thankful for some of the things you *don't* have, like a broken arm or worse. Look around and you will see all kinds of people with all kinds of problems you *could* have, but don't.

    Now the question is this: Which list do you think about the most? Do you spend more time being thankful for what you have or wishing for things you don't have? Too often, we choose to focus on what we don't have, especially when others around us seem to have more. We begin to feel sorry for ourselves, to be envious or angry. Helen Keller had every

Thoughts That Count

reason to feel sorry for herself after a childhood illness left her blind and deaf for the rest of her life. Instead, she chose to be thankful. "So much has been given to me," she wrote, "I have no time to ponder [think about] that which has been denied."[1] That spirit of thanks giving helped Keller to become one of the most successful writers and public speakers of her time, and one of the most admired women in American history. We can all make the same choice she made, the choice to be thankful for what we have—whatever we have.

So keep your wish list, your hopes, and your dreams, but don't forget to give thanks for what you already have. And don't forget to show your appreciation to those who have helped you. How many of them, near and far, deserved your thanks today, but didn't get it? Tomorrow is another day, another opportunity to remember them—in your thoughts and with your actions, a kind word, a thank-you note. Thanksgiving is one day of the year, but thanks giving is an everyday thing, a habit, a way of life. Start each day with thanks giving and end each day with thanks giving, giving thanks for what you have, and for what others have done for you.

W – O – R – K

**The world doesn't owe you anything;
you'll have to work for what you want.**

Go ahead. Find yourself a nice, comfortable chair. Before you sit down, grab a soft drink or two, a bag of chips, maybe a sandwich. Then sit back and wait.

Sit back and wait for the world to bring you everything you ever wanted, everything you think you deserve. Maybe you would like to make better grades than any of your classmates, learn to play a musical instrument, or be a quarterback on the football team. Maybe you're in a new school and just need to make some friends. What would you like to be when you grow up? An artist? An architect? A carpenter, a counselor, or a college professor? Maybe you would rather pitch in the World Series or make it big in Hollywood. Do you want to be rich, own a big house or a million dollar automobile? And what about those things money can't buy, like respect and love? No doubt, you would like those as well. Whatever it is you want or want to be, just have a seat, get comfortable, and wait for the world to bring it to you. And wait, and wait, and wait...

No one survives the first years of life without the care and protection of others. Without that care and protection, probably from one or more parents, you wouldn't be here today. But the responsibility of early caregivers to help you *decreases* as your ability to help yourself *increases*. Are a lot of good people willing to help you even now? Of course—when you really need it. But they, too, will expect you to help yourself whenever you can. After all, why should *anyone* care about the needs of a spoiled kid sitting in an easy chair making demands? Truth is, if you sit around waiting for others to bring you what you want, you are going to be *very* disappointed.

Thoughts That Count

The good news is that most of us don't have to wait. We can get out of our comfortable chair, turn off the television, and start working for whatever we want.

"Work" isn't just another four-letter word. It is just about the *only* way we can make our dreams come true.

So, decide what it is *you* want most, develop a plan, and get to work. You won't get everything you want; none of us do. But if you are patient, keep working, and don't allow yourself to quit or become distracted, you will be amazed at how much is possible.

The choice is yours. Sit back and wait for someone to give you what you want, or get up and work for it. If you choose to sit, get ready for a long, long wait. The world doesn't owe you anything; you'll have to work for what you want.

One Now, or Two Later?

**Getting what you want later means giving up
some of what you could have now.**

What is your favorite candy treat—a Snickers bar? A Butterfinger? A pack of M&M's? A Reese's Peanut Butter Cup? Now imagine that someone put one of your favorites in front of you, and offered this choice: eat it now, or wait until later. If you choose to wait, you will earn a second treat just like the first. Could you wait? For how long—a few minutes? A few hours? Meanwhile, as you wait, the first candy bar waits with you, begging to be eaten. What choice would you make, one treat now or two later?

When we are very young, we want what we want—and we want it NOW! The idea of waiting has no appeal to us. Imagine trying to talk a hungry baby into waiting for his next bottle. But as we grow older, we begin to realize that some of what we want *most* cannot be so easily or quickly gained. Want a good report card? You won't get it the first day of school. Want to save enough money to buy a new bicycle? That could take months. How about a college degree? That will take years. Would you like to become a professional athlete or walk on the moon? Perhaps you can—someday. But all of these, and just about everything else you might hope to accomplish, take time—days, weeks, months, sometimes years.

Of course, we do not get what we want simply by waiting. We must work while we wait. A good report card requires many hours of homework and study, day after day, throughout the school term. You won't earn the money for a bike playing video games or taking a long nap. You will have to work for it. College degrees aren't handed out to just anyone who shows up at graduation. They require the successful completion of one class after another, until all requirements have been met. Professional athletes

Thoughts That Count

develop their skills in countless practices and games before ever being paid for their efforts. Becoming an astronaut? That may be even harder.

So, gaining the things you want most takes time—and work. Anything else?

Yes, you will have to give up some of what you could enjoy now—like not being able to eat the first candy treat while waiting for the second. Making good grades probably means giving up time in front of the television or computer. Saving your money for a bike or for college means NOT spending your money on all the other things you might like to have in the meantime. Time spent practicing your athletic skills or working to become an astronaut means less time hanging out with your friends. The greater the prize, the more you will have to give up to earn it.

Life is constantly giving us choices, something now, or something better later—one treat or two. Children who always get what they want when they want it never learn the importance of working for what they want and waiting to get it. Of course, some of us never learn. But if we don't, we are likely to be disappointed with what we are able to accomplish and what we are able to gain.

Are you willing to wait? Are you willing to work hard in school every day in order to get a good grade at the end of the term? Are you willing to save your money until you have enough to buy the things you want? Are you willing to give up some of what you could have now in order to get something better later? Who knows? Someday, if you wait long enough, work hard enough, and give up enough treats, you might even own the factory—the candy factory, that is. Think of it: a giant mound of your favorite treats—all yours.

Byron Wesley Lehman

Little Red Wagon

Pull your own little red wagon; pull your share of the load.

Little red wagons have been a part of childhood play for as long as any of us can remember. Of course, wagons today are a little fancier than before, and not all of them are red. In a good wagon, an imaginative child can carry just about anything to just about anywhere. When very young, many of us can expect an occasional free ride, pulled by an older and stronger family member or friend. But as we grow older, the free rides gradually end, and we begin to realize that our wagon isn't going anywhere unless we pull it ourselves.

Life is a never ending list of things to be done that are much like pulling a wagon—from cleaning house to paying bills, from raking leaves to raising a family, from opening a lemonade stand to owning your own business, from helping a younger brother or sister to helping a neighbor or defending your country in time of war. The question is, in your family, your school, your country, when an important job needs to be done, who does it? How many are helping to pull, and how many are just along for the ride, content to let others do all the work?

Some of us really *can't* help. The very young are not yet able to pull their share of the load. And some are too sick or too old to pull as once they did. But others are just too lazy. They add extra weight to the wagons others must pull. When times are good and our wagons are rolling merrily along, we may not look around much to see who's helping to pull. But when life becomes more difficult and the road ahead is all uphill, we begin to notice who's helping and who's not. At such times, we need everyone pulling who can.

How about you? Are you doing your share of the pulling—at home, at school, with your friends, in your community? Or do you expect others to do all the work for you? The world needs all the wagon pullers it can find—not just those who are strong, but those with a better plan, those who are brave, those who can lead, those who encourage others. They, too, help to move the wagon forward. So, if you aren't already doing your share of the pulling, get to work. If it's your mess, clean it up! If it's your job, do it! If it's your problem, don't just complain about it, find an answer. Sure, you will need help sometimes, but growing up means learning to do more and more for yourself. The real world offers opportunities even greater than those we imagined as a child. We really can travel anywhere on Earth (and far beyond). Our dreams really can come true. But first, we have to grow up and stop expecting others to do the work for us. Everyone else is counting on you—to do what you can, to pull your own little red wagon, to pull your share of the load.

The Cookie Jar

Give at least as much as you take.

Regardless of age, most of us are cookie snatchers at heart. We simply love reaching into an unguarded cookie jar and SNATCHING fresh baked treats.

Now think of the world as a giant cookie jar into which we all reach for the many things we want and need. We all like to take, of course, but how much are we willing to give back? Ask yourself questions like these: "Do I usually take all I can get and give as little as I can get away with?" "Do I give as much to others (my family, my friends) as they give to me?" "Is my class better when I'm *at* school, or when I'm not?" "If I had a job, would I be worth every penny I was paid?"

Now a story: Long ago there was a rich businessman who tried to help people whenever he could. One day, when a man came asking for help, the rich man showed him a box filled with money. "Take whatever you need," the rich man offered. The visitor emptied the entire box, leaving nothing behind. He promised to repay the rich man, but, of course, he never did. Several years later, the visitor found enough courage to return to the rich man and ask again for help. "Sure," the rich man said, showing him the same box as before, "Take all that you need." The man looked in the box, only to find it empty. "There is nothing there!" he said. "Of course there is nothing there," the rich man replied. "If we take, but put nothing back, there will be nothing left to take." [2]

So, during your lifetime, will you give back to the world at least as much as you take? Will you put more cookies into the jar, or take more out?

Byron Wesley Lehman

Thoughts That Count

Me-ville

Leave Me-ville behind; think "we," not "me."

Regardless of where we are born, we all begin life in the same place, a place called Me-ville, where life is all about ME. As newborns we are full of demands. When we are hungry, we let everyone know. When we want to be held, we want to be held NOW. Our entire world consists of little more than a bottle of milk, a diaper change, a pacifier, a soft bed, and someone to care for us. If our needs are being met, our world is good, but our world is also very small.

We don't yet know or care about the needs of others—whether Mom has had enough sleep, whether everyone else in the family has been fed. We know nothing about the needs of the family down the street. We have no idea that we share the planet with about seven billion other people.

While Me-ville can be a great place to begin life, the problem is that some of us never leave there. Even as our understanding of the world grows, we continue to care about no one but ourselves, never understanding that the universe is bigger than Me. Strangely, most of us know someone like that, but just about none of us would ever admit being that person ourselves.

We humans were not made to live apart from others, but *with* others, sharing the good times and the bad, caring about others as they care about us, loving and being loved in return. What could be worse than winning a race, making the best grade on a test, seeing Niagara Falls or the Grand Canyon—and having no one with whom to share the experience? That would be like being the only person invited to your own birthday party. You would have the whole cake to yourself, but how much fun would the party be? What could be worse than suffering a great loss and having no

Thoughts That Count

one to comfort you? But who will care about your suffering if you have not first learned to care about theirs?

Working together, we can accomplish great things, like winning the soccer league championship, finding the cure for a deadly disease, or landing a human being on Mars for the first time. If you are lucky, you will experience the great joy of being part of a successful team. But you will never find that joy in Me-ville.

Leaving Me-ville doesn't mean that your needs are to be forgotten or ignored. It means finding a better place, a place where your concern for others leads others to be concerned for you, a place where everyone's needs can be met.

Yes, we are all born in Me-ville, where we care only about ourselves. But we are also born with a built-in need to leave Me-ville behind, to go beyond ourselves, to experience not just our own home front, but the rest of the world as well. The sooner we reach beyond ourselves, the more interesting life becomes for us, and the more interesting we become to others. If you still live in Me-ville, open your front door and walk out into the great world that awaits you.

What's Your Excuse?

Don't make excuses; take responsibility for your actions.

Emma has talent, all kinds of talent. Just ask Emma. She will tell you that she could have played the lead role in the school play, but her teacher didn't like her. She could have been the best player on the soccer team, too, but she didn't have time for all those silly practices. She could have made a high grade on last Friday's test, but she wasn't feeling well that day. Emma can do just about anything, but no one like her ever gets a chance. She can explain away any failure or broken promise—and always find someone else to blame. Maybe you know someone like Emma. Maybe, just maybe, you are a little bit like her yourself.

If you want to know all there is to know about making excuses, just ask a kid—someone like Emma, perhaps, but just about any kid will do. Adults make plenty of excuses, too. But kids are more creative, more imaginative. How many reasons have *you* used for not having done your homework, for leaving a mess in the kitchen, or "forgetting" to do your chores? Have you ever been "too sick" to go to school, only to feel much better the rest of the day at home?

We make all kinds of excuses for doing what we know we shouldn't, or *not* doing what we know we should. We find reasons to explain our failures, as though we never really had a chance in the first place—the color of our skin, our family or neighborhood, the way we look...We tell ourselves that we are not big enough, strong enough, smart enough, talented enough, rich enough. Rather than admitting our mistakes and accepting responsibility for our actions, we find someone else to blame. Instead of looking within ourselves for answers to our problems, we expect someone else to find answers for us.

Thoughts That Count

And who among us has *ever* had a better excuse than Helen Keller? A childhood illness before the age of two left her unable to see or hear, and she remained without sight or hearing for the final eighty-five years of her life. Did she feel sorry for herself? Or give up? Did she use her condition as an excuse for doing nothing, being nothing, achieving nothing? Not a chance.

Though she lived the rest of her life in a world few of us can imagine, she graduated from college. She became a writer whose books have been translated into more than fifty languages. Incredibly, she learned to speak, lecturing in more than twenty-five countries.[3] She spoke about, wrote about, and defended her beliefs. By just about any standard, she was a great person.

Of course, Keller did not achieve greatness entirely on her own. She was fortunate to have a loving family and many friends, like Annie Sullivan, her teacher, and Polly Thompson, her secretary. Alexander Graham Bell, who invented the telephone, also played a role in Keller's development. But for all their help, they could not give Helen Keller what most of us simply take for granted—the ability to see and hear.

Sometimes we just want to sit back and swap sad stories with someone like Emma, making one excuse after another for every failure, every mistake. Then along comes someone like Helen, whose life makes a lie of *all* our excuses. She overcame every hardship life threw in her path. Can we not do the same? So now, what's *your* excuse?

Byron Wesley Lehman

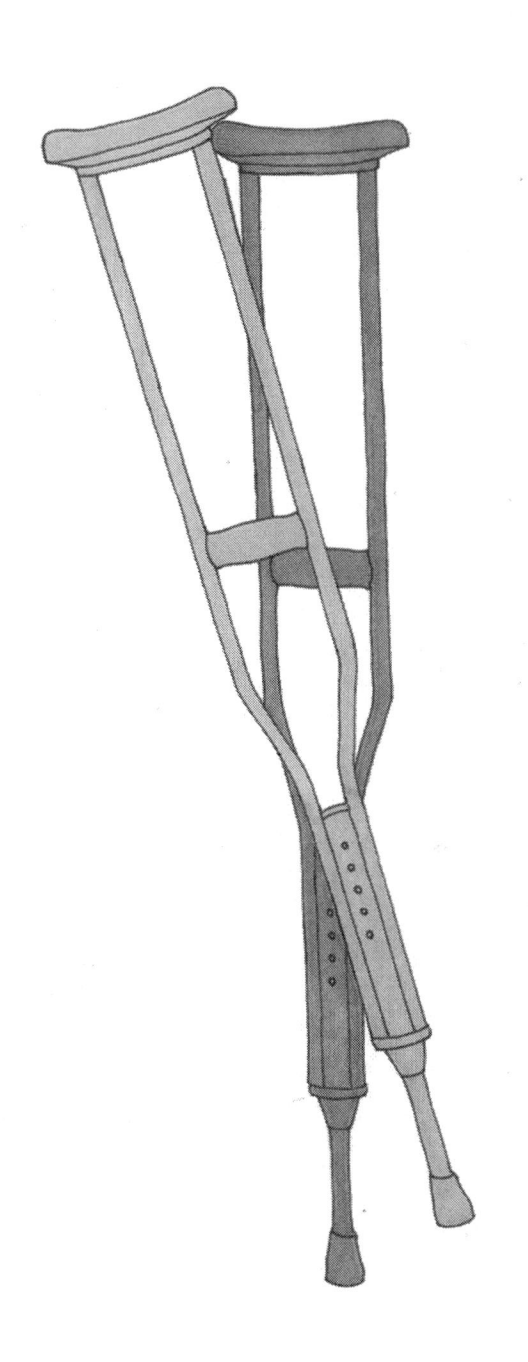

Treasure Hunt

If you are in search of hidden treasure, look within.

If you were to go in search of treasure, where would you go? Would you need a map? Would you look at the end of the rainbow, as some have suggested? Would you dig in the sands of some distant island? So many places to look, and so little time.

Years ago, an eight-year-old boy named Jim, while living on a farm in Missouri, found an old coin—a very old coin larger than any we use today.[4] At first, he really liked his new, old coin, but soon he lost interest in it, put it in his junk box, and pretty much forgot about it.

Years later, Jim, by then an adult with bills to pay, pulled out his old coin and began to wonder...Could it actually be worth something? So, he took his old coin to an expert. Turns out it was more than five hundred years old (very old indeed), and it was worth...well, no one knew for sure, but the expert thought it might be worth as much as $500,000 (in other words, a *lot* of money).

Now think, what if *you* had found that coin instead of Jim. Wow! That would be great, right? But what if you had put that coin in your junk box and left it there for the rest of your life? What if you *never* learned its value, *never* knew how "rich" you really were? What a waste that would be.

Now think again, what if the treasure you held so long wasn't an old coin you had found, but an undiscovered talent inside you—mechanical, mathematical, musical, whatever it might be. What if you were capable of greater courage and heroism than you ever imagined? What if you could influence the world in ways you never thought possible? Wouldn't it be sad if you lived your whole life without ever making use of these undiscovered talents, without ever knowing just how "rich" you really were? Could that happen? You bet. It happens all the time. How many great writers, how many artists, how many leaders pass through life without ever discovering that special talent within themselves? How many of us could have been this, or could have done that, if only we had discovered and developed the treasure within? The truth is, there is more to each of us than meets the eye—more to us than even we ourselves can see.

Jim's good fortune may be nothing compared to your own, if you look for treasure where it can certainly be found—within you. A great wealth of inner strength, talent, and potential lies within you even now, waiting to be discovered and developed. So, if you are in search of hidden treasure, look within. You might be amazed to learn just how much you are worth.

Thoughts That Count

Hard-to-do Things

Doing hard-to-do things makes you stronger.

Hard-to-do things come in all sizes and shapes. Some are harder than others—like running a marathon, more than twenty-six miles. Imagine how hard that would be. But each year about twenty-five thousand runners attempt the Boston Marathon, and nearly all of them finish the race. Rather walk instead? Why not join those hiking the Appalachian Trail from one end to the other, from Georgia to Maine, a distance of more than two thousand miles? Your journey will take months to finish, but each year hundreds finish the trip.

You may never run twenty-six miles or hike two thousand, but if you are to live a full life, doing hard things will be a part of it. Getting a college degree is hard. Becoming a doctor is even harder. Making your dreams come true, becoming the best at whatever you do, being a good person, the person you really want to be, becoming a respected leader—all of these are hard, too.

Are you ready for such hard-to-do things? When we are young, most of us aren't. But great accomplishments are never accomplished easily, so how *can* we get ready to do the really hard things that offer many of life's greatest rewards? The answer is simple: by facing and overcoming lesser challenges, and growing each time we do. The best preparation for doing hard things is doing hard things. If you aren't ready yet to conquer the most difficult challenges, tackle one not quite so hard—like riding your bike up a steep hill, or getting along with a brother or sister. How about finishing a school project *before* the last night, changing a bad habit, or learning to tell the truth, even when a lie would be easier to tell? Admitting your mistakes, continuing to try when you feel like giving up, facing a bully at school—all of these are hard, but you can do them. The

Thoughts That Count

problem is that too many of us do everything we can to *avoid* things that are hard—things that make us uncomfortable, make us work, or make us think. We don't understand how important hard-to-do things can be, and how they make us stronger in every way.

We don't improve our math skills by working the easy problems over and over. We don't learn to get along with hard-to-get-along-with people by never being around them. We don't learn to be brave by avoiding every risk. We don't build muscles by lifting weights that are easy to lift. Teams don't improve by playing only the teams they can easily beat. Doing only what is easy just doesn't prepare us to do what is hard.

Even if it were possible to live our entire life doing things that are easy, we really wouldn't want to. A full life includes struggle as well as rest, with plenty to challenge us and force us to grow. Of course, life doesn't always give us a choice. It has a way of placing hard-to-do things in our path, uninvited things like being separated from a loved one, dealing with an accident or illness, or losing a job. At such times, we may be thankful for all the bumps and bruises that came before, the tears and pain, the unkind words, the struggles, disappointments, embarrassments, and defeats—all the hard things that made us stronger.

If a younger brother or sister is driving you crazy, welcome the chance to grow patient and caring and kind. If you are having trouble in your math class, welcome the chance to learn and to grow. A hard-to-do thing is our best teacher. It builds our character and strengthens us for the far greater challenges ahead. And, strange as it may seem, hard-to-do things—the most demanding, the most challenging part of our journey through life—are often the things we remember with the greatest pride and joy. Think about it: What is the hardest thing *you* have ever done, and how do you remember it today? Give thanks for the hard-to-do things. Find something hard to do and *do* it. Who knows? Maybe one day you *will* run in that marathon, hike the Appalachian Trail from one end to the other, or better yet, see your dreams come true.

Swing the Bat

Success begins with the courage to risk failure.

Nothing great or small is ever accomplished, no victory ever won, no home run ever hit, until someone with courage overcomes the fear of failure and decides to try.

Imagine for a moment any of the great hitters of baseball with a pitch approaching them at 95 miles per hour. The batter swings—and misses. Ever happen? Of course. Hank Aaron and Babe Ruth, two of the greatest hitters of all time, combined for 1,469 home runs, but they struck out nearly twice as often. How many of their home runs came after a swing and miss on the previous pitch, or a strikeout in the previous at bat? No doubt many. Even great hitters play for days (sometimes weeks) without hitting a home run, but they seldom experience a time at bat without taking a swing. Their willingness to accept the risk of missing, and missing again, makes possible their extraordinary success. And when their playing days are over, we remember their hits, not their misses.

To ride a bicycle for the first time is to risk falling. To ask a question in school is to risk being laughed at. To try out for the team or the school play is to risk failure. To express an opinion is to risk criticism from someone who doesn't agree. Love is always a risk, among the greatest of all. Courage doesn't come to us all at once. Courage starts small and grows a little at a time—with each swing of the bat, with each opinion expressed, with each attempt to do what we have not done before—so that one day we will be prepared to face far greater challenges.

Before taking any risk, the wise person considers what can be gained, what can be lost, and the chance (or likelihood) of success. Not all risks are worth taking. But though fear may keep us from doing foolish things we shouldn't, it can also keep us from attempting what we could. Too

Thoughts That Count

often we are unwilling to accept even the risk of a missed swing or the laughter and criticism that might follow. It is much better to go without a hit than to go without a swing.

Can you remember a time when you had the courage to take a risk? Can you also remember a time when you lacked the courage to take a risk you now wish you had taken? Success begins with the courage to risk failure and criticism. Give success a chance. When opportunity comes your way, swing the bat!

Get Back Up!

When I fall down, I get back up.

After watching the Olympics on television, two brothers, ages four and seven, decided to create a running event in their own backyard. They would jump over three well-spaced "hurdles," circle around a nearby tree, and return, jumping over the same three hurdles again before reaching the finish line. For hurdles, they had chosen matching monster trucks and a dump truck. Eager to show his grandfather the new course, the younger brother set out at full speed. But as he attempted to jump over the final monster truck, he tripped and fell. Pulling himself up, the four-year-old assured his grandfather that he was OK. "When I fall down," he added wisely, "I get back up."

Though we don't like to think about it, life is full of *falling-down* experiences. Sometimes we lose. Sometimes we fail. Sometimes we are disappointed. We don't always get what we want or accomplish what we had hoped to. Every day we make mistakes. None of these are a pretty sight. What if you had a home video of your most memorable falls? How graceful would you look? Well, the falls of an Olympic ice skater are no better. But no matter how often they fall, no matter how damaging a fall has been to their chance of winning, skaters are trained to get back up, control their emotions, and finish their routine. It's hard to do, but they do it, time and time again. So can we.

No one learns to ride a bicycle without falling. The number of falls doesn't matter much, as long as we get back up each time we fall, and eventually learn to ride. Falls are the price we pay for the joy of riding, and for most of us, riding is worth the price. The Wright brothers built the first successful airplane, but not on their first try. They failed and failed again, but they kept getting back up and trying again, until at last they changed the world. Willie Mays is remembered as one of baseball's all-time greatest hitters. But when he first arrived in the major leagues, he had no hits in his first twenty-one times at bat. Today those failures are of no real consequence when compared to the success that followed. The price of success nearly always includes failure, but failure doesn't have to be the final chapter.

Living life to the fullest requires that we journey into the unknown, beyond what is comfortable, familiar, and certain. On such a journey we are sure to experience failure, sure to make mistakes—many of them. Even the greatest among us do. And, from time to time, we are sure to slip and fall. Woops, there goes another one! But the rewards of such a life make the trip worthwhile and the risk worth taking. Successful people aren't those who never fall, but those who get back up when they do, learn from their mistakes, and keep on trying—again, and again, and again, until at last they succeed.

Dragons

Somewhere there's a dragon with your name on it, a purpose waiting to be found, a need waiting to be met—by you.

Some people believe in good dragons. So from the beginning, let's make one thing clear. We're not talking here about good dragons. We're talking about bad ones, fiery, people-eating dragons, the kind you wouldn't want to meet in a dark alley. Dragons like that have stalked their way through storybooks for hundreds of years and probably will for hundreds more.

Long ago, just such a dragon lived in a cave at the foot of a mountain. One day a group of children who lived nearby were playing knights and dragons just outside their castle walls. As children sometimes do, they ignored their parents' warning to stay near the gate, and began to stray further and further from the safety of the castle walls and closer and closer to the dragon's cave, until finally they found themselves face-to-face with the fiery monster himself. At this point, the children were hopelessly cornered, except for Kaleb, who, because he always lagged behind the others, had not been seen by the dragon. When Kaleb saw the danger to his friends, he quickly ran for help.

Even before Kaleb had reached the castle, his cries for help were heard by Sir Render, the knight on duty at the time. At this particular castle, Sir Render worked the knight shift, which meant he was available whenever needed. Now, Sir Render wasn't exactly like the other knights. As you might have noticed, even his name was a little strange, though it wasn't always so. At birth he was given the name Render McWright, but when he became a knight, the queen gave him the title Sir, and, as they say, the rest is history. Now, Sir Render wasn't the best looking knight you ever saw, or the biggest or the strongest. But everyone agreed that he was

Thoughts That Count

a knoble knight—kind and kourageous. And whenever anyone had kneed of a knight, Sir Render was always ready to do what knights do best.

When Sir Render heard Kaleb's call, he wasted no time. Some knights take days just getting on their armor, but Sir Render was ready in a blink. By the time the boy reached him, he had already gathered up the old sword his grandfather left him and somehow mounted his horse. (Perhaps you have never actually seen a knight in full armor trying to mount his horse, but one day you really should.)

When Sir Render heard the boy's story, he quickly turned his horse and rode gallantly toward the cave. As he rode, he remembered the times when, as a boy, he sat on the castle walls at night, gazing at the stars and thinking about the heroic acts of service he would one day perform. He hadn't always known that he would be a knight, but he somehow knew that he was on this Earth for a reason, that he had work to do, and that he would do that work well. "I was made for just such a time as this," he thought to himself as he neared the cave. "Even a knight cannot do everything, but what I can do, I will. I must!"

Sir Render reached the cave just in the nick of time, and courageously stepped into the path of the approaching dragon. To make a long story short, when the dragon saw Sir Render, he charged right at the noble knight, with a most un-neighborly look on his face. But at the last possible moment, Sir Render stepped aside, raised his sword and...well, some things are better left unsaid. But let me assure you, what happened next was not good for the dragon, and this particular dragon would never again threaten innocent children.

We all like stories with happy endings (happy, except for the dragon). But our story continues. Today we are threatened by dragons as never before, though most are not of the fiery type faced by Sir Render. Today's dragons come disguised as hatred or hunger, as a terrorist, a murderer, or a thief, as homelessness, addiction, or disease. Indeed, the number of "people-eating" dragons seems to grow by the day. To make matters worse, knights in shining armor have nearly disappeared from the face of the Earth. (When was the last time you saw one on your street?) So, if the dragons of today are going to be slain, someone is going to have to take up where the knights left off—that's us, that's you—young and old, male and female, all are needed. Seldom will we need a sword and shield, though warriors are still necessary from time to time. More often we will need a medicine kit, a toolbox, a knitting needle, a tractor, a book, a kind word of encouragement, the gift of time to someone in need—our weapons are as varied as the dragons we now face.

During your lifetime you will have many dragons to slay, some more important than others. But if at the present time you see no dragons, keep looking—life would be boring indeed without dragons, without purpose. Somewhere there is a dragon with your name on it, a purpose waiting to be found, a need waiting to be met—by you. And if you don't slay that dragon, who will?

Thoughts That Count

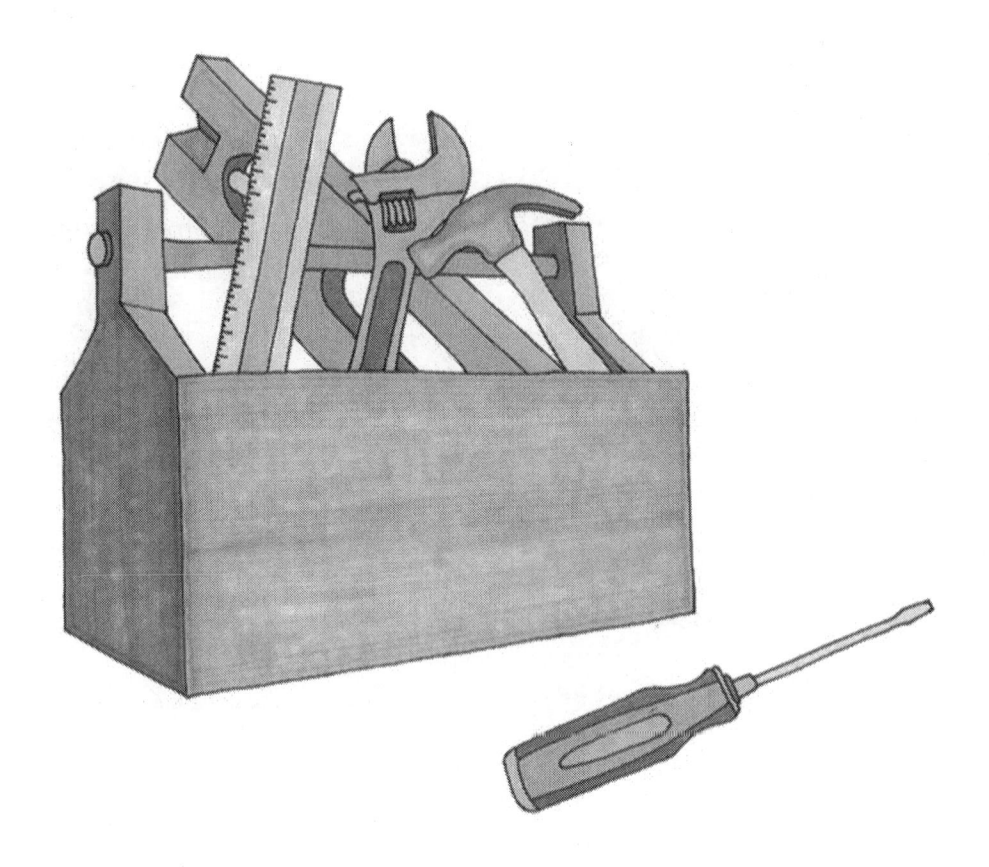

The Toolbox

No one has all the tools; build with the tools you have.

Even an average size toolbox can hold many treasures—tools of all sizes and shapes, including some whose use we can only guess. But did you know that each of us has a different kind of toolbox that is entirely our own? In that box we carry all of our talents, all of our skills, everything we have ever learned, the strength of our character—in other words, all of the "tools" we have to solve problems and accomplish all things great and small. Have work to do? You can do it—if you have the right tools. Some people, of course, have more tools than others, but *no one* has all the tools, and *everyone* wishes he or she had more. The problem is that we complain way too much about the tools we don't have and make way too little use of the tools we do have.

We have all looked at someone and thought, if only I were like him, as smart as he is, as handsome, as fast, or as strong. If only I had what she has—good parents, a nice home, new clothes. If only I were as old as this person or as young as that one. At the same time, someone, somewhere is looking at us and thinking how great life would be if they had what we have. Oh, how happy we would *all* be and how great our accomplishments would be, if only...Or so we think.

Edward R. Sill[5] once wrote a poem about an "if only" kind of guy. In his poem he describes a scene, perhaps real, perhaps just dreamed, in which a furious battle rages.

We hear the sounds of men screaming and swords clashing. In the middle of the battle, nearly surrounded by his enemy, a prince, the son of a king, courageously fights for his life. Meanwhile, at the edge of the battle a coward bitterly complains about the quality of his sword. If only he had a sword like the prince, he tells himself, he too would fight with great courage. Angrily he breaks the blunt sword he has, throws it to the ground, and creeps away from the battlefield. Moments later, now badly wounded and without his weapon, the prince, standing where the coward once stood, sees the broken sword. Quickly, he pulls it from the sand, returns to the thick of the battle, and leads his men to victory and, as the poem concludes, saves "a great cause that heroic day."

The coward in our story is not unusual. Even those of us with many, many tools often leave the battlefield of life without ever having used them. We become discouraged; we make excuses—the color of our skin, the school we attend, the neighborhood we come from, any excuse will do. After all, we may not be a prince or belong to a family of wealth. We may not be the smartest in our class, the most popular, or the most athletic. We may not be the best at *anything*. So, we complain about the tools we have, wish for better tools, and *do* nothing.

The truth is that few of the world's great builders have been from the richest families. Few have been the smartest in their class, the most popular, or the most athletic. Most have been more like us, with tools enough—enough to do incredible things, more than they could at first imagine. And the tools they lacked, they worked to get.

The problem with the coward wasn't the strength of his sword, but the strength of his character. He lacked the confidence, determination, and courage of the prince to use what he had, even a broken sword left in the sand. You, too, can live a heroic life and serve a great cause if you act courageously, with confidence and determination. But you can't do anything until you stop feeling sorry for yourself, set aside your fears and excuses, and get to work. What matters most isn't the number of tools in your box, but what you build with the tools you have.

Light One Candle

**Light one candle and then another,
helping those in need—one by one by one.**

Every child experiences some sadness and pain. But some of us are more fortunate than others. We experience childhood without suffering, hunger, or homelessness, without having to battle a life-threatening disease. We have someone who cares about us and cares for us. But as we grow older, we become more aware of those less fortunate, those who have suffered greatly and, perhaps, lost hope. Many of us then ask what we can do for them. But when we see their numbers and how great their needs can be, we begin to doubt our own ability to help. Indeed, the problems of the world *are* great, and none of us can solve them all. So what *can* we do?

Many years ago, a young Albanian girl named Agnes began a journey that would change the world. After becoming a nun, Agnes went to India, thousands of miles from her home and family. At first she was a teacher. But eventually, the suffering she witnessed led her to live and work among those who needed her most, the poorest of the poor—the hungry, the sick, the dying. Her approach was simple. When she saw a person in need, she tried to help. If a baby was hungry, she would go for milk. If a family had no bread, she would provide them bread. If a man was dying, she would comfort him until he died. To those who reminded her that she could do so little when compared to the great need all around her, she would say, "I do not think the way you do...I only subtract from the total number of poor or dying." "Ek, Ek, Ek," she would say, which meant, "one by one by one." Soon, others followed her example and their work spread to country after country, making a difference in the lives of millions of the world's most needy. Years later, Agnes, by then known around the world

Thoughts That Count

as Mother Teresa, was awarded the Nobel Prize for Peace. Even today, long after her death, thousands of others continue her work, assisting those in need "one by one by one."[6]

The needs on your street or in your neighborhood probably aren't as great as those Mother Teresa found in other parts of the world. But you would not have to go far to find people in need. What will you do? Turn away and pretend you didn't see? Become discouraged and lose hope? Wish that someone would do something to help, but do nothing yourself? Or will you actually *do* something? That "something" could be helping your mother, especially when she is tired, caring for a younger brother or sister, being a friend to the new student at school, helping to feed the poor, a simple thank you, a word of encouragement, an act of kindness.

You cannot do everything, but you can do something. You cannot help everyone, but you can help someone. You can light one candle and then another, helping those in need—one by one by one.

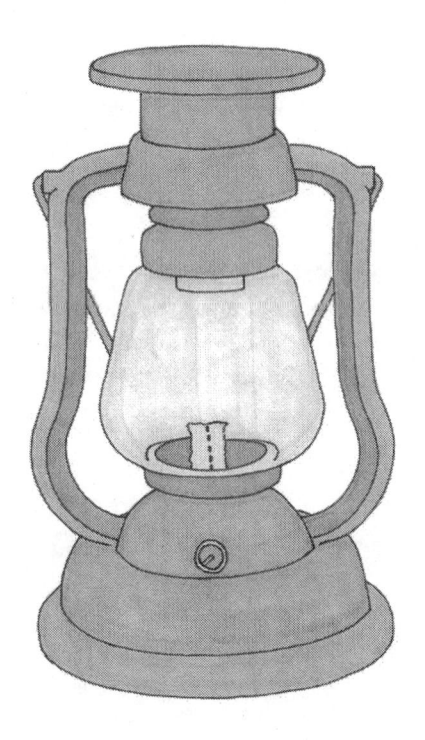

Superheroes

Ordinary people are capable of extraordinary, heroic accomplishments.

Aaron and Alisha could barely believe their eyes. Quite accidentally, they had stumbled upon a plot to destroy the entire city, perhaps even the world. Time was running out. But what could two kids possibly do to stop the evil-doers? In an instant they knew. They would seek the help of someone with superhuman strength, someone faster than a speeding bullet, someone whose pursuit of justice never ends, someone like... Superman.

Who is your favorite superhero? Spider Man? Wonder Woman? The Teen Titans? Captain Marvel? Batman? However dangerous, however impossible the task, superheroes like these have always been there to save the day—at least in comic book and television fiction. But in the real world, no superhero, not even Superman, has ever saved *anyone* from *anything*. Too many of us do not understand that when the world has a need, it has only us to call upon, "ordinary" people who look more like the mild-mannered Clark Kent than like Superman, people who can't even see through walls, much less leap over tall buildings, ordinary people who, when the need arises, act in extraordinary ways to accomplish whatever must be done.

Abraham Lincoln was born in a log cabin in the wilderness—nothing "super" about that. But he was just the right man to lead his country through difficult times. Clara Barton's fellow students never thought of her as a superhero. In fact, they probably didn't think much of her at all. Though she was extremely bright, she was shy, and had few, if any, friends in her early school years.[7] But what a hero she must have been to the Civil

Thoughts That Count

War wounded whose lives she saved and to those who have since been served by the American Red Cross she founded.

Acts of courage and kindness occur every day—millions of them. Some involve risk and a whole lot of courage. Who are the people who do these things? Are they all straight-A students or members of the football team? Are they all among the most popular students in their school? Are any of them ten feet tall? Of course not, and none of them can fly. Most are just ordinary people, a whole lot like you, who see a need and try to meet it. But to the people they help, they must seem like Superman or Wonder Woman.

Superheroes make great fiction, but when real problems need to be solved, when real people need real help, ordinary people will have to get it done, people like Aaron and Alisha—and you. Can you do it? Of course you can. You are exactly the right person for the job. You don't have to be bigger or stronger than anyone else. You don't need to have superhuman powers or abilities. You don't even need a costume. You just need a big heart, a sense of justice, and enough courage to do what needs to be done. And each time you do what needs to be done, the "hero" inside you grows a little stronger, more capable, and more courageous. So get to work. The world needs heroes, lots of them. The world needs you. There is *so* much to be done.

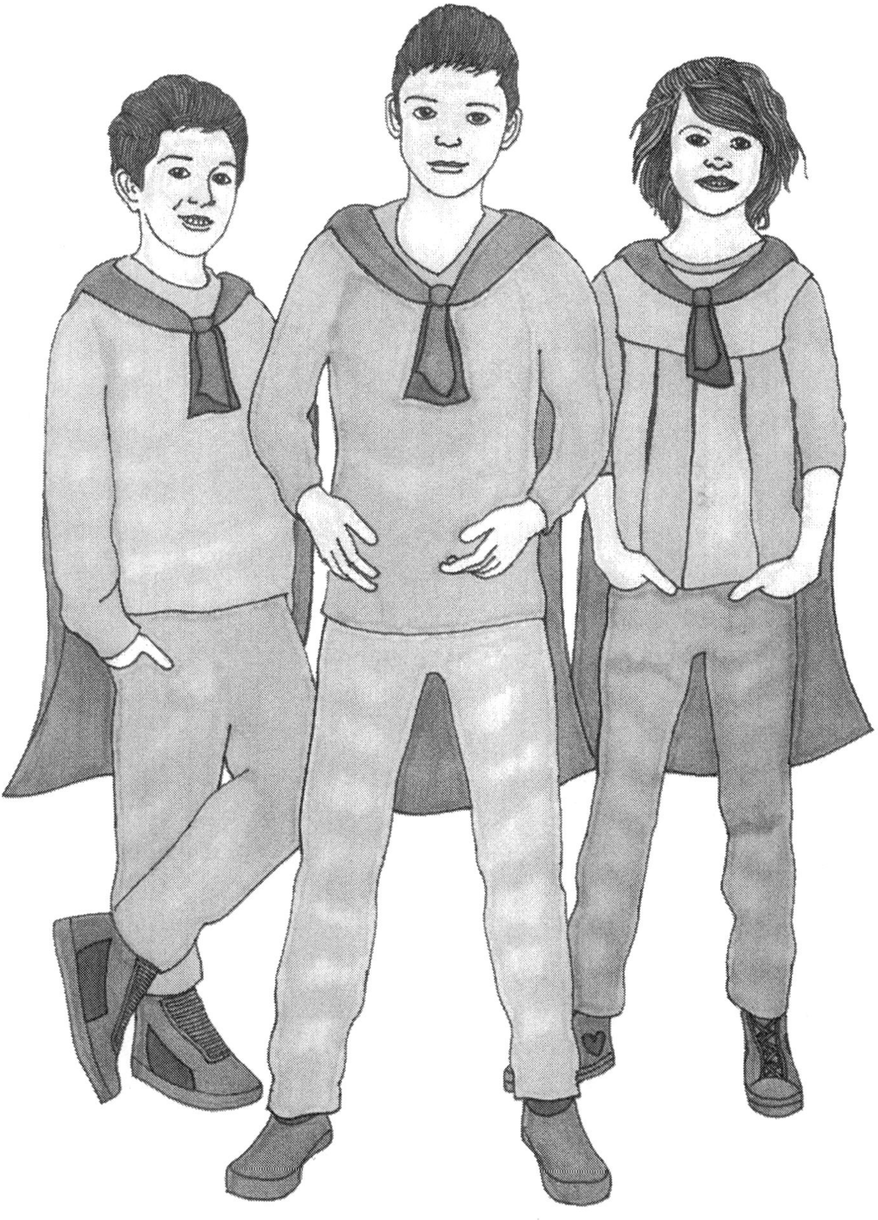

Baby Steps

The steps you take today determine your tomorrow.

Olivia was just over a year old when she took her first steps. For weeks, even months, she had been preparing. She had crawled. She had "walked" while holding the hands of her mother and father. She had learned to stand and balance herself, if only for a moment. She had watched others walk, especially her older brothers, and noticed how much faster their movements were than her own. Then, one day it happened—step, step, step, without even knowing what she had done. Soon she was walking everywhere, and getting into everything. Though she doesn't remember those first steps, they made possible every step she has taken since.

Every person who has ever run the Boston Marathon and every person who has ever won an Olympic gold medal in track began his or her running career the same way—with a first step, just like Olivia. In 1969 Commander Neil Armstrong became the first person to step foot on the moon. "That's one small step for man," he said at the time, "one giant leap for mankind." But even that historic step began with steps taken many years before. We call them baby steps, and though no one remembers the moment, everyone who has ever walked began that same way.

When we are young, most of us have someone we look up to, someone who has already accomplished things we, too, hope to accomplish one day. We see them as heroes or role models. What we don't always understand is how they got where they are, and, more importantly, how we might be able to get there ourselves. No one achieves greatness overnight, but over time, step by step. An ice skater doesn't begin his career in the Olympics. Years of practice and lesser competitions come first, with no guarantee of success. A doctor doesn't begin her education in medical school, but in elementary school, like everyone else. A president makes countless decisions, both great and small, before ever reaching the White House. No one acts with great courage who has not already acted with a little courage.

Never underestimate the importance of what you are doing now. The steps you are taking *matter*, no matter how small or wobbly they might be. If you are going in the wrong direction, even baby steps will get you in a lot of trouble quicker than you can now imagine. But if you are going in the right direction, keep going. Never think the distance is too great to attempt. Not every dream comes true. Not everything is possible. But for most of us, far more is possible than we ever dreamed. We *can* accomplish great things, but great things are not accomplished in an instant. We begin at the beginning and work our way to the end, one step at a time. Want to make a big difference? Want your life to really matter? Start by making a little difference, and go from there. Even baby steps can get you closer to where you want to be. So remember: the steps you take today determine your tomorrow.

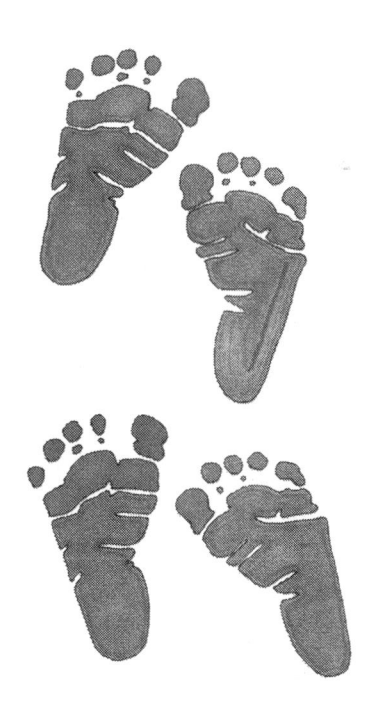

Promises

**Make only the promises you can keep,
and keep the promises you make.**

Babe Ruth was one of the greatest baseball players of all time. Some say he was *the* greatest. In 1927 he set the major league record for home runs in a single season, a record that lasted thirty-four years. But to this day no one has ever matched what he is said to have done as a New York Yankee in the 1932 World Series. While batting against the Chicago Cubs in the fifth inning of a 4-4 game, Ruth appeared to point to the center field bleachers, as if to say he was about to hit a home run in that direction. On the next pitch he did just that. No one before or since has ever "called" a home run before hitting it. Some say Ruth didn't either, that the purpose of his pointing had nothing to do with the home run that followed. But, true or not, the story of Babe Ruth's home run that day will be remembered as long as the game of baseball is played. He did what he said he would do.

If you want to be different, to stand out somehow from others, try this simple formula: make only the promises you can keep, and keep the promises you make. Your actions may not be remembered as long as the Babe's home run in 1932, but like him, you will be seen as a one of a kind person. One of a kind? Don't most of us keep our promises? Take a closer look. Many of us mean well. The problem is that we promise too much. We promise in order to get someone "off our back," or because we want someone to like us. But without thinking, we promise too much, and when the time comes, we are unable or unwilling to do what we have promised. So, part of the answer is to think more, and promise less. Sometimes the answer is to make no promise at all. You will be much better off *not* making a promise than making one you cannot, or will not, keep.

Sometimes we tell ourselves that some promises don't really matter. No one will notice or remember them. But in the eyes of others, *every* promise matters, however big or little it might seem at the time. When was the last time an adult made a promise to you but failed to keep it? Did you forget? Well, no one is going to forget your broken promises, either. So, when you say, "I'll take out the trash," take out the trash. When you say, "I'll call you," call. When you say, "I'll be there," be there. Every time you keep a promise, no matter how unimportant it may seem, you make it easier for others to trust you, even when it matters most.

You don't have to be Babe Ruth or promise a home run. Just do what you say you will do. Anyone can do that—but few of us do. That's why people who *can* be trusted and *do* keep their promises stand out in the crowd. Be one of them. Make only the promises you can keep, and keep the promises you make.

Size of the Dog

Big dogs don't have to bark.

No one knew for sure what kind of dog Shakespeare was, but one thing everyone knew—he was a *big* dog. While enjoying a spring walk with his owner, Shakespeare suddenly spotted a nearby dog less than half his size. For just a moment, each stopped in his tracks and looked at the other. Then the small dog began to bark. Unimpressed, Shakespeare turned away and continued his walk. By the time he and his owner had returned home, Shakespeare had crossed the paths of several other barking dogs, but the big guy ignored them all, moving ahead proudly, nose held high, happy to be who he was, and where he was. Such walks were always the highlight of Shakespeare's day, and he would not allow them to be ruined by the tiny yappers he met along the way.

Perhaps you have seen Shakespeare on his daily walk, or a dog like him—a dog so self-confident, so content with himself, he didn't have to worry what the other dogs were doing or "saying."

Perhaps you have also seen *people* who are a lot like Shakespeare, not because they are physically bigger than those around them, but because they are big inside—self-confident, secure, and at peace with themselves. Such people are slow to anger, slow to be offended, slow to have their feelings hurt. Having no need to put others down in order to make themselves look better, they are slow to criticize or point out mistakes.

They have no need to brag, no need to exaggerate their own accomplishments, no need to prove themselves to others or seek their approval. They seldom worry what others are thinking or saying about them. Because they are content with their own lives, they have no need to be jealous of anyone else's. Because they are pleased with their own success, they don't feel threatened by the success of others. Because they are secure within, they can show concern for the needs of others. In other words, with little need to be defensive, they are free to be themselves. Does this description remind you of anyone you know? Would it remind anyone you know of you?

In responding to others, you always have a choice. Just because someone is barking at you, you don't have to bark back. (OK, people don't really bark...or do they?) Just because someone is trying to make you angry, you don't have to be angry. Just because someone wants to hurt your feelings, you don't have to let them. Dr. Richard Carlson puts it this way: "If someone throws you the ball, you don't have to catch it." He goes on to suggest that you have the same choices when responding to an unkind word—"catch it and feel hurt," or "drop it and go on with your day."[8] The bigger you are inside, the more choices you will have, and the easier it will be to just "drop it and go on with your day." Like Shakespeare, you can let the little yappers yap, and continue to enjoy your day, your way. Truth is, some things *are* worth fighting for, but some things aren't. The choice is yours. Consider the cost before making your choice. Remember: big dogs can bark whenever they want, but they don't have to.

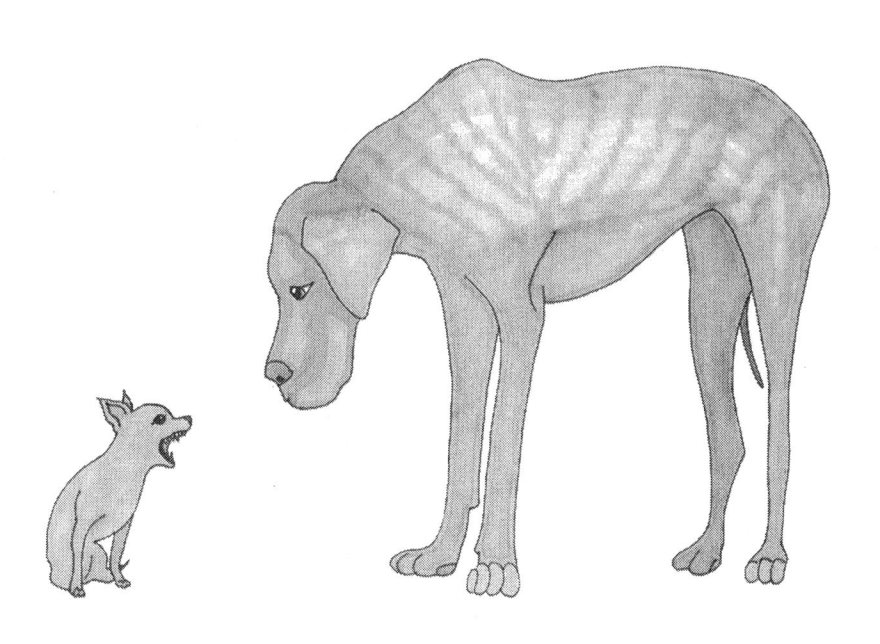

Cheerleader

Encourage others.

Cheerleaders—go to just about any high school or college sporting event and you will see them supporting their team. Watch them for just a while, and you will see how athletic they are and how hard they work to perfect their routines. Do cheerleaders make a difference? Of course they do. We all do better when others are there to support us.

Perhaps *you* would like to be a cheerleader. Then again, maybe you would rather keep your feet on the ground than be thrown high into the air while hoping someone below remembers to catch you. Maybe you prefer soft drinks and chips to somersaults and cartwheels. Maybe those uniforms really aren't your style.

Most of us will never wear a cheerleader's uniform. But we can all become cheerleaders of another kind—without the uniform or the crowd, or even the back flips. We can all be the kind of person who encourages everyone around us, and does so day after day. We don't have to be chosen for this team of cheerleaders; we make the choice ourselves. And the world can never have too many of us. In fact, it never seems to have enough.

And what do we cheerleaders without uniforms do? When someone is successful, we celebrate their success. When someone's confidence needs a boost, we encourage them. When someone is sick, we comfort them. When someone is discouraged, we give them hope. When someone suffers a loss, we do what we can to cheer them. We give high fives, we show respect, we listen. Rather than finding fault with others, we find something to praise. We remember our thank-yous. We show our support, our appreciation, and our confidence in others.

As cheerleaders without uniforms we never miss a chance to make others smile or feel good about themselves—a check-out worker at our local grocery, a school bus driver, a fellow student, a food server at the school cafeteria, a parent, brothers and sisters, teachers, and friends. Even those who seem to have everything will value a kind word. And remember to save a few cheers for yourself.

To encourage others, you don't need a uniform and you don't need to be the smartest or most talented person in the room. Anyone can do it, but most of us don't. That's why those of us who do are appreciated so much. Occasionally, someone will tell you how much your words of encouragement have meant. Most of the time, you will never really know. But many of us have been changed forever because somewhere, sometime, someone believed in us and took the time to tell us so. You, too, can make a difference in the lives of those around you, just by giving the gift of encouragement—a gift of great value that costs nothing to give. Give it often. Give it now. Encourage others.

Invisible

How many invisible people have you "seen" today?

Have you ever wondered what would happen if you could somehow flip a switch and become invisible, if only for a while? Think of the mischief you could get into without fear of being caught! What a story you would have to tell! But then, how would you feel if you decided to become visible again, and the switch no longer worked? Now that's scary!

Unfortunately, many of us already *feel* invisible, a kind of invisibility no one would ever choose. We get that feeling when no one seems to notice us, when no one seems to care about us or appreciate what we have done, when no one even tries to understand us. With a little thought, we could probably all make a list of invisible people that we know. Let's try.

We will call the first person on our list Mr. Walker. Mr. Walker drives the school bus, though a lot of the kids on the bus don't notice. They must think the bus is driven by remote control. But everyday Mr. Walker gets them safely to school on time and safely home—with very little thanks, to be sure. Meanwhile, Mrs. Walker works in the cafeteria at school, where lunches magically appear day after day, prepared by an entire crew of invisible people—invisible, at least, to most of the students they serve. The Walkers are only two of the countless people who make a difference in our lives, often without our noticing—from those who collect our trash, to those in our military who risk their lives every day in foreign lands just to keep us safe at home.

Now let us meet another invisible person, Ariana, a hungry six-year-old on a continent far away. Of course, she is surrounded by other boys and girls who are no better off than she. Though we don't want to think about them, and have never actually seen them, we know they are there.

Ariana could also be a neighbor recovering from an accident, the victim of a tornado or flood, a child who is sick—any person in need. The world is filled with such people, often through no fault of their own. If we look, we will see them, perhaps for the first time.

Chances are we all know yet another invisible person. We will call him Michael, though many of us know him by a different name. He is a student in our school, perhaps even in our class—the one who doesn't fit in, the loner, the uninvited, the last person chosen, the one whose work goes unnoticed, despite his best effort. If we cared enough to look, we could find someone like Michael in almost any setting. Even when surrounded by others, Michael feels alone. Like so many others, Michael isn't the most athletic, the most attractive, or the most outgoing. He never gets elected to...well, anything. But years later, many of those like him grow up to be successful, sometimes famous. You may have overlooked him once, but doesn't Michael deserve a second look, and a little respect?

Sometimes *we* are the invisible ones. Have you ever felt left out, like you don't fit in? Were you ever the child who raised her hand all day long but was never called upon by her teacher? Have you ever expressed your opinion and received no response, as though you had not even spoken? Have you ever seen those around you greet one another with enthusiasm, while barely noticing when *you* walk into the room? Have you ever felt like you were...invisible? For some of us, these things happen every day. For nearly all of us, they have happened enough so we can remember how we felt at the time. What would it mean to you if someone took the time to discover who you are, and what makes you so unique, so special? What would it mean if someone actually listened to what you had to say, tried to understand you, enjoyed being with you?

Invisible people are everywhere, and, believe it or not, they aren't hard to find. Learn to be grateful for what so many of them have done for you. Begin to see their needs, as you have never seen them before. Show respect for their hidden talents and potential. If, at the moment, you are feeling a bit invisible yourself, find the courage to talk with someone you

Thoughts That Count

would like to know better—especially if that person is also invisible. Just imagine: two invisible people being visible to each other. Wouldn't that be something! How many invisible people do you know? How many invisible people have you "seen" today?

The Real World

Learn to live in the real world

Have you ever dropped a coin into a wishing well or fountain, made a wish, and believed (or hoped) that somehow your wish would come true? Many of us have. Have you ever seen *The Wizard of Oz*? Remember those shoes Dorothy was given? She clicked her heels together three times, said the magic words, and BAM—she was back home in Kansas. How about *Aesop's Fables*? Have you read the one about a goose that laid golden eggs? Who wouldn't want a goose like that? Maybe you have also read about Cinderella, and the Fairy Godmother who turned a pumpkin into a coach and mice into horses, so that Cinderella could ride to the ball in style. If you haven't read about Paul Bunyan and his blue ox, Babe; Batman; and Wonder Woman, well, you probably will. And who hasn't heard of that guy named Harry (Potter, of course) and his magic wand?

At one time or another, nearly *all* of us have read or watched our way into the world of fiction and fantasy. It is a great place to visit. The problem is that too many of us try to live there.

The world of fantasy and fiction is a world of unlimited opportunity, where anything is possible. But some things you just can't do in the real world. Cows can't jump over the moon, money doesn't grow on trees, and *you* can't fly like Superman. Nor can you *have* everything or *do* everything that *is* possible. You will have to make choices—which movie to watch, which musical instrument or sport to play, what you would like to be when you grow up. In the real world, you won't always be able to do what you want, or get what you want. No one does. Understanding that makes living in the real world a lot easier.

In the real world, you'll have to work for what you get. Want to be rich someday? Maybe you can be, but don't waste your time looking for a golden goose. Want to be like your favorite professional athlete or movie star (or any other successful person you know)? If so, no wave of Harry Potter's magic wand will get you there. You'll have to learn the "how-to" behind their success—the goal setting, the hard work, and the sacrifices they were willing to make. Their success didn't come overnight, and it didn't come easily. Maybe you want to be like someone your own age who can do things you can't. Maybe that person is physically stronger, or better at math. Maybe he makes friends more easily. Maybe she can play a musical instrument, paint, or draw. Why can't you be like that? Perhaps you can be, but wishing wells and magic words won't make it so.

In the world of fantasy, consequences seldom exist. That's why an action hero can be shot at all day long without ever being hit. (Don't try that one at home.) Fantasy world thinking allows us to believe we can do just about any foolish thing, involve ourselves in all kinds of destructive behavior (like alcohol or drug abuse), without suffering the consequences. Characters on television and in the movies do it all the time. Perhaps for a while we can, too. Then one day, reality kicks us in the back end, and we wish we had listened to all the warnings. In the real world, behavior does have consequences. We can't treat others poorly and expect them to treat us well. We can't earn their trust while telling them lies, even "little" ones.

So, enjoy reading fantasy and fiction if you want, but don't confuse fantasyland with the world you live in. Click your heels together as often as you like, but be prepared to find another way to get where you want to go. Learn to better understand the real world—what is possible and what is not, what works and what doesn't, what helps you accomplish your goals, and what could hold you back. Learn who can be trusted to teach you, and who can't. Learn to "see" the consequences of your actions before you act. Pay attention to what is happening around you. Whether you like it or not, the real world is the world you must live in. Learn to live there.

Byron Wesley Lehman

The Same Boat

We are all in the same boat.

As free people, we have an important question to ask: Why should we care what happens to anyone else? Or as they might ask, why should they care what happens to us?

Consider the following, long-ago story told about three men floating downstream in a small boat. None of them could swim. Suddenly, a very strange thing happened. One of the men began to cut a hole in the bottom of the boat. When the others realized what he was doing, they were shocked, and ordered him to stop. "Mind your own business," he told them. "I am boring a hole under my seat only, not under yours."

"Yes," the other two replied as with one voice, "but if you continue, we will all be drowned, for we are all in the same boat."[9]

Like the man in our story, we would like to believe that what we do is no one's business but our own. But is it? None of us rides through life alone; we wouldn't want to. We have family, friends, and neighbors. We form teams; we join groups. We live in communities and nations. If we really are in the same boat, don't we have a responsibility to everyone else in the boat? A bad choice by any one of us can affect everyone else. A bad decision or careless mistake can cause a team to fail, damage the reputation of an entire family, or sink everyone in the boat.

When we begin to care about those in the boat with us, something else happens. They begin to care more about us, and we become more effective as a "team." Great accomplishments are seldom the work of one person acting entirely alone. No one person built the house you live in or the car you ride in; teams built them. Even the most talented players can't win a Super Bowl or World Series alone. Teams win, or teams lose—together. Our success, our happiness, even our survival depend on our ability to work together with others who share our goals, goals none of us could hope to achieve alone.

So, why should I care what happens to you? And why should you care what happens to me? Because we are all in the same boat; or as others have said, we are all riding through the universe on the same ship, Spaceship Earth.[10] In ways we don't even realize, our actions affect one another. What you do affects me; what I do affects you. Our words can encourage and inspire, or bring pain and the loss of hope. We can help each other achieve our goals, or we can hold each other back. We can build, or we can destroy. We can make each other's lives better, or make them worse. Think about some of the ways you affect those around you. And remember—we reach our destination together or we sink together, for we are all in the same boat.

Under Construction

Your country needs *you*—we all have work to do.

Just about everyone likes to complain. How about you? In a free country like the United States, we can, you know. At any given time, about half of us don't like our president, and no one ever likes to pay taxes. At one time or another, most of us have complained about the public schools, and at this very moment someone is complaining about a pothole on his street that needs to be fixed, NOW! We expect a lot, and we get a lot, though never quite as much as we expect. The problem is that we too often ask what our country can do for us, rather than what we can do for our country.[11] We act as though the United States was built long ago, finished and done with, here to serve our every need. In truth, the building of America never ends, our country remains a nation "under construction," and now *we* are the builders.

On July 4, 1776, the thirteen original colonies of the United States declared their independence from Great Britain. The Declaration of Independence signed that day assured the right of every American to "Life, Liberty, and the pursuit of Happiness." But it was only the beginning. Before construction of a new country could move forward, a war of independence had to be fought. Many of the fifty-six signers of the Declaration of Independence paid a dear price for their freedom. Some lost their fortunes, or saw their homes destroyed in the war; some were captured and imprisoned by the British; more than few lost their lives. But in 1781, the British army surrendered to the Americans at Yorktown, and the colonies were free.

In 1787 a new constitution was written by men including George Washington, Ben Franklin, James Madison, and Alexander Hamilton. Our Constitution, still in use today, established the rights of every American and the laws by which we live, while promising "a more perfect Union." But perfection hasn't been easy to achieve. Twenty-seven amendments have since been made. Some changes came quickly, others, more slowly. Slavery wasn't ended until 1865, and women didn't gain the right to vote until 1920.

In 1861 the Civil War divided our country into North and South. More than six hundred thousand died in the fight. But when it was over, the country was united again. Then came World Wars I and II. Nearly a million Americans were killed or wounded in those wars, but evil had to be stopped. It was, and our freedom was protected at home, and restored to countless others around the world.

Can one person make a difference? Our history offers countless examples. Elizabeth Blackwell was a difference maker, the first female doctor in the United States. She was turned down by a number of medical schools before finally being accepted at a school in New York. In 1849 Blackwell graduated first in her class, paving the way for others to follow. Today, almost half of all students admitted to medical schools in the United States are women.[12] Dr. Martin Luther King made a difference, too. In the 1950s and '60s, he led a peaceful "revolution" for the civil rights of African Americans. His work ended the separation of races in schools and other public places.

Perhaps you have already read about the rise and fall of some of the world's great empires, such as the Greeks, Romans, Incas, and Aztecs. For a time, each ruled much of the world as they knew it. But in time, each empire fell. None of them exist today, though we can still see their influence. The United States is the greatest, most powerful nation of our day. But for how long will its greatness continue? Only so long as each new generation of Americans does whatever must be done to defend it and make it better.

Today, the work of building our nation continues. At times we have made a mess of it all. But if we are to become "a more perfect Union," we are the ones who must clean up whatever messes remain. One person *can* make a difference. *You* can make a difference. Get the best education you can get. Learn as much as you can about the world you live in. Grow stronger—in every way. Build your character and leadership skills. Help someone in need. Begin to consider what your role might be in the continued construction of this great country.

So, complain as much as you like, but remember this: this country has been built by the labor and sacrifices of millions. Now it's your turn. If we are to remain a free people, if we are to become a better, more just society, we all have work to do. *You* have work to do. Your country needs *you*.

Rearview Mirror

You are responsible for what you leave behind.

Even if you are too young to drive, you are not too young to learn one of the most important rules of driving: keep your eyes on the road ahead. That is good advice for all of us, whether we have four wheels beneath us, two wheels, or none. But as we travel through life, we also need to peek every now and then into the rearview mirror to see what we are leaving behind.

A quick look at just about any street or highway reminds us of the litter left behind by some, as they drive or as they walk. Empty drink bottles and cans, cigarette butts, candy and food wrappers, and a whole lot more—you have seen it all, and it isn't a pretty picture. Strangely, much of the litter comes from people who live in the neighborhood. Perhaps they think, "Just one wrapper won't matter." More likely they don't think at all, or think only of themselves. They never look into their rearview mirror to see what they have left behind.

Some of us take that same careless lack of concern for others into our homes. When we are finished making a mess in one room, we move on to the next, without ever looking back to see what we have left behind. Empty glasses and drink cans, snack wrappers, plates and bowls, school papers, toys—we leave it all behind, as if we have no responsibility for our own messes. Someone else is supposed to follow along behind, cleaning up the messes we have made.

A look back into our rearview mirror can reveal more than litter on the street or a messy room. At times we might see someone we could have helped, but didn't. With a closer look, we might even see someone whose feelings have been hurt by our cruel actions or words. We could see them, if we cared enough to look.

Thoughts That Count

Of course, some of us can look back with pride. John Chapman had no rearview mirror as he walked across the frontier over two hundred years ago from Pennsylvania to Illinois. If he had, he would have seen apple orchards blossoming where once he had walked and planted apple seeds. He would become known as "Johnny Appleseed." Loving mothers and fathers can look back with pride at the children they have raised; doctors, on the patients they have helped; teachers, on the students whose lives they changed. All kinds of people can make a difference and look back on a world they made better, if only a little.

As we look into our own rearview mirror, we might also check out who's following us. Like it or not, we are being watched. And no matter how good or how bad our example might be, others will follow it. Take a look and see if it isn't so.

What about you? What does a room look like after you have passed through it? Do you clean up your own mess, or leave it behind for others? What do people look like after you have passed through their lives? Are they better or worse for having known you? Is someone watching you and following your example? Go ahead; take a look now. What do you see in your rearview mirror? Remember, you are responsible for what you leave behind.

Byron Wesley Lehman

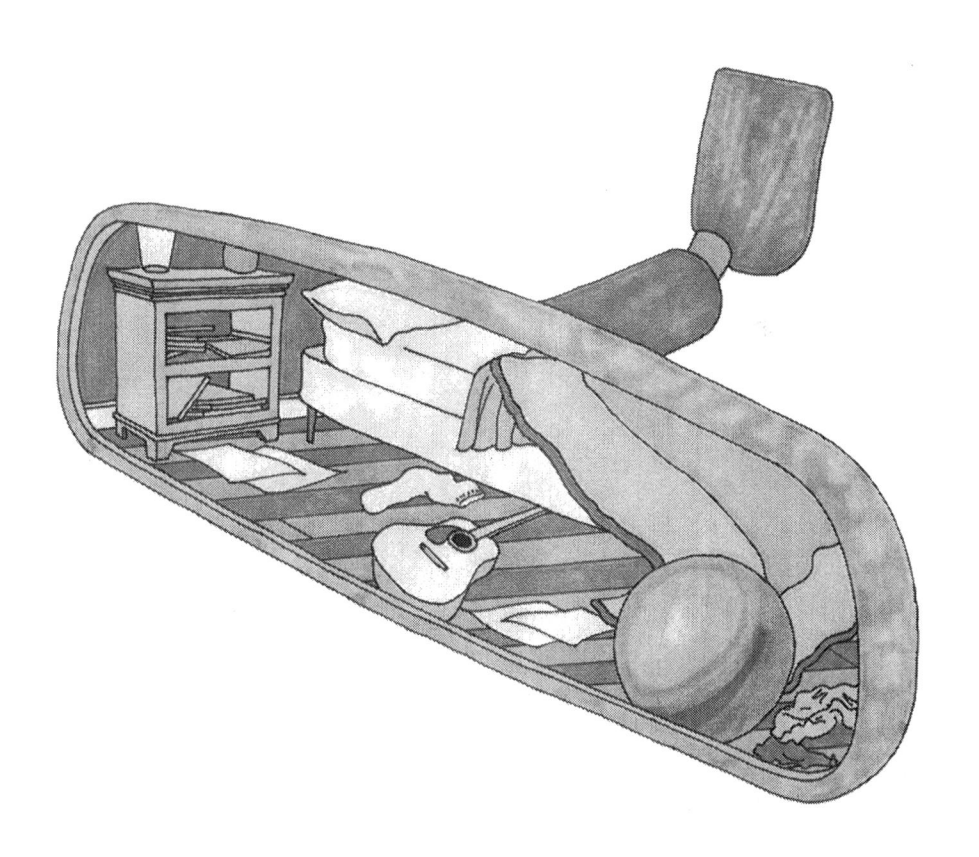

About the Author

The late Byron Lehman spent many years working on this "project" that has now come to fruition in print entitled Thoughts That Count. Our family is excited to publish this book to honor an amazing man who truly wanted to make a difference in this world. He is well remembered as being a coach, a teacher, a business owner and a loving, proud husband and father of four. Byron was a lifetime St. Louis Cardinals baseball fan and a huge Kansas Jayhawks basketball fanatic. He was quick-witted, generous and wise. He believed in Luke 12:48 that reads "To whom much is given, of them much will be required."

Notes

1. Helen Keller, quoted in Sean Covey, *The 7 Habits of Highly Effective Teens* (New York: Simon and Schuster, 1998), 57.
2. Marva Collins, *Values: Lighting the Candle of Excellence: A Practical Guide for the Family* (Los Angeles: Dove Books, 1996), 181–182.
3. "Helen Keller Biography – "Life Is Either a Daring Adventure or Nothing"" *Amillionlivesnet Rife with Life*. N.p., n.d. Web.
4. Associated Press, Old Medallion may be Worth $500k, *Northeast Mississippi Daily Journal* (Tupelo, MS), March 31, 2001, 1.
5. Edward R. Sill, "Opportunity" *The Little Book of American Poets: 1787-1900*. Ed. Jessie B. Rittenhouse. Cambridge: Riverside Press, 1915.
6. Kathryn Spink, *Mother Teresa: A Complete Authorized Biography* (New York: HarperCollins Publishers, 1997), 257.
7. Elizabeth Brown Pryor, *Clara Barton: Professional Angel* (Philadelphia: University of Pennsylvania Press, 1987), 11.
8. Richard Carlson, PhD, *Don't Sweat the Small Stuff...and it's all small stuff* (New York: Hyperion, 1997), 219–220.
9. Abraham Cohen, *Everyman's Talmud: The Major Teachings of the Rabbinic Sages* (New York: E. P. Dutton, 1949), 184.
10. Adlai Stevenson (Speech to the Economic and Social Council of the United Nations, Geneva, Switzerland, July 9, 1965). "We travel together, passengers on a little space ship, dependent on its vulnerable reserves of air and soil."
11. John Fitzgerald Kennedy (Inaugural Address, January 20, 1961). "And so, my fellow Americans: ask not what your country can do for you—ask what you can do for your country."
12. Nancy Groves, "From Past to Present: The Changing Demographics of Women in Medicine: http://www.aao.org/yo/newsletter/200806/article04.cfm

Made in the USA
Charleston, SC
05 May 2016